HOW TO BE PERFECT

How to Be Perfect

BY RON PADGETT

COFFEE HOUSE PRESS

Minneapolis

COPYRIGHT © 2007 Ron Padgett
COVER ART "Goldfinch," by C. Fabritius, Royal Cabinet
of Paintings, Mauritshuis, The Hague
AUTHOR PHOTOGRAPH © John Tranter
COVER + BOOK DESIGN Coffee House Press

Coffee House Press books are available to the trade through our primary distributor, Consortium Book Sales & Distribution, www.cbsd.com. For personal orders, catalogs, or other information, write to: Coffee House Press, 79 Thirteenth Avenue NE, Suite 110, Minneapolis, MN 55413.

Coffee House Press is a nonprofit literary publishing house. Support from private foundations, corporate giving programs, government programs, and generous individuals helps make the publication of our books possible. We gratefully acknowledge their support in detail in the back of this book.

Good books are brewing at coffeehousepress.org

LIBRARY OF CONGRESS CATALOGING-IN-PUBLICATION DATA

Padgett, Ron, 1942–
How to be perfect / by Ron Padgett.
p. cm.
ISBN-13: 978-1-56689-203-2 (alk. paper)
ISBN-10: 1-56689-203-1 (alk. paper)
I. Title.
PS3566.A32H67 2007 811'.54 DC22
2007017772

3 5 7 9 8 6 4 2
Printed in the United States

ACKNOWLEDGMENTS

Thanks to the editors who published some of these poems in their magazines and webzines: *Aerial, Blackbox, Coconut, Green Mountains Review, Lemniscata, Metrotimes, Partisan Review, Pataphysics, The Sienese Shredder, Shiny, Vencil,* and *Verse.*

"Thinking about the Moon" appeared as the text of a handmade limited-edition book by Anne Walker, "Now You See It" in a catalog for an exhibition by Alex Katz at Pace Wildenstein Gallery, and "Sketch" in the 2003 annual of the Civitella Ranieri Foundation.

Special thanks to the Civitella Ranieri Foundation for a residency fellowship in Umbria, where some of the poems in this volume were written.

Hats off to everyone at Coffee House Press.

To my grandson
Marcello Padgett
and his parents
Wayne and Siobhán

Contents

Mortal Combat

You can't tell yourself not to think
of the English muffin because that's what
you just did, and now the idea
of the English muffin has moved
to your salivary glands and caused
a ruckus. But I am more powerful
than you, salivary glands, stronger
than you, idea, and able to leap
over you, thoughts that keep coming
like an invading army trying to pull
me away from who I am. I am
a squinty old fool stooped over
his keyboard having an anxiety attack
over an English muffin! And
that's the way I like it.

Rinso

The slight agitation
of pots and pans
and a few dishes
in sudsy water
into which hands
plunge and fingers
operate like in
a magic act in which
bubbles burst
into flowers presented
to the blonde girl
who rotates on
a wheel that flies
up through the
ceiling and
disappears.
The dishes
are sparkling.

Tops

When I was little I had a top
that spun on its point.
A lot of kids had tops,
I guess they spun them.
The tops went round and
around—but?
(The mystery
of centrifugal force?)
My top slowed down and
went crazy-wobble, and I
got up and spun
and staggered dizzy,
flopped and threw
the spin into the floor.

The Swiss Family Robinson

I never quite understood who
the Swiss Family Robinson were.
The inversion of their name
confused me at an early age,
just as the name of Mary Baker Eddy
sounded as though she started out
as a woman and turned into
a guy named Eddy. At Walt
Disney World there is an attraction
called Swiss Family Robinson that
involves a tree house, so I assume
they lived in a tree. Why they did
I don't know. It sounds rather
stressful to me, the fear
of falling out. I could look up
the Swiss Family Robinson
in a reference book, but
it's interesting not to know
something that everyone else knows.
However, I *would* like to know if there
are many people named Robinson
in Switzerland. If there are,
I would know something that
most people don't know.

Blizzard Cube

I'm going out to see the blizzard
that is approaching in the form of a cube.

I am in a children's book
where a blizzard won't hurt me.

After I have experienced the blizzard
to the fullest, to the very core of my being,

I will return to the house,
my head wrapped with the bandages

I put there to keep my brain inside my skull.
Later I will take them off, revealing

my mouth enough to tell you what
it was like inside the blizzard cube,

assuming, of course, that you will still
be there and interested.

Rialto

When my mother said Let's go down to the Rialto
it never occurred to me that the name Rialto

was odd or from anywhere else or meant anything
other than Rialto the theater in my hometown

like the Orpheum, whose name was only a phoneme
with no trace of the god of Poetry, though

later I would learn about him and about the bridge
and realize that gods and bridges can fly invisibly

across the ocean and change their shapes and land
in one's hometown and go on living there

until it's time to fly again and start all over
as a perfectly clean phoneme in the heads

of the innocent and the open
on their way to the Ritz.

Everybody and His Uncle

I was waiting to happen.
At a stoplight
the buildings curved up from my ears,
office buildings
with offices in them and people
doing office things, pencils
and paper clips, telephone rings—
Where is that report?
At Echo Lake the vacationers
have made the city only slightly
emptier, how did they get there?
By station wagon and dogsled
in the "old" days. The forest ranger
was Bob. He said we could spell his name
backwards if we wanted, then
our laughter vanished into his tallness.
I thought maybe he was not a forest ranger,
just a guy named Bob, but
it turned out he was part of the echo
of everything around there, which radiated
out a few short miles before the farmland set in.
The farmland had waited to happen
and then it did, just as it knew it would.
A farmhouse appeared and a front porch
and on it sat my Uncle Roy. He was very farmer.

"Get on this horse," he said.

But the horse said, "Don't."

"I would prefer to play baseball," I said.

Later we took Rena Faye to the hospital.

"Darn that horse," Roy said, "when his ears

laid back I saw trouble." The light changed,

my shoes went across the street

while I rose straight up into the high part of the air

so as to form a right angle

with the dotted line that lit up behind my shoes

as they turned into pots of gold

receding into that smaller and smaller thing

we call distance. But I was already there

in the distance, I had been waiting my whole life

to be wherever I should be at any given moment,

a ring around not anything. "Wake up, Rena Faye,"

said Roy, "we need to take you to the hospital."

She gave us the most beautiful smile

but it bounced off our faces and we forgot

to pick it up and put it somewhere safe.

It's probably still lying there on the road

in front of the house. Come to think

of it, I did pick mine up

as I looked out the back window of the car,

and as we skirted Echo Lake

everything got twice as big and then three times,

like laughter and hiccoughs flying among children

whose immortality has turned them

into temporary rubber statues of curvature in confusion
that slides into the appeasement of early evening.
That is, Rena Faye felt better, at least she was able
to know there was a bump on her head, and inside
the bump a small red devil running furiously in place.
"Rena Faye is going to be okay," said Roy,
but I wasn't so sure, there was a doctor involved
and a hospital with a lot of white in it.
The house hadn't changed, but the barn
was gone and the land stretched out flat
to far away. The horse was still waiting, for what
who knows? I was waiting at the light, and when it changed
I went on across the street
to where another part of town was waiting,
it was Europe and I was in or on it,
I had Europe touching my foot, the train
was pointing its big nose toward the Gare St-Lazare,
where you wake up even if you aren't asleep.
Rena Faye opened her eyes and said, "I don't think . . ."
and then a funny look
came across the street toward me, the one big horrible face
of surging forward, but I was like whatever bends
but doesn't break because I didn't give a whit about any of it,
I was in the forest and my name was almost Bob and the trees
didn't care about any of it either because tallness can't care.
Roy wasn't really my uncle, we just called him that.
When the sun rose his new picture window could be seen through
to the lone mimosa tree, its pink blossoms smiling frizzily,

and a car went by, not a Chevrolet or a Ford,
not a green or blue car,
just a car, with a person driving it. My notebook
and its pencils were ready to go and I
moved toward them as if music had replaced the sludge
we call air. I.e., Swiss cheese had become Gruyère.
The car started, then rolled back and stopped.
We got out and looked, then kicked ourselves. Moon,
is that what that is, that sliver? I was thinking,
the car was not thinking, my pencils were almost thinking,
all three of them, but they took too long and so
time went on ahead without them.
Then an angel from the side touched my head inside
and my head outside surrounded less and less.
His wristwatch is a street, green, yellow, blue, and open
as a meadow in which your parents are grazing
because the fodder and forage are stored away
in the kitchen cabinet too high for them to reach
with their muzzles. And lo the other parents are mooing
plaintively, tethered to an idea they like to dislike:
The fox is free. Silly old cows, the fox is never free,
he is just running, and with good reason, and with good legs,
from the ooga-ooga. Brrrrring!
Waterfall of afternoon!

And I left.
I went east three miles and then
fifteen hundred more, and then

three thousand five hundred more,
and then I turned around
and came back five thousand and no hundred.
My mother was still in the kitchen
standing on the yellow tiles
as dinner rose up out of the pots and pans
and hung in the air while she adjusted it.
Soon Dad came home and we dined
but he didn't and neither did Mother
and neither did I. We put the food
in our mouths and chewed and swallowed—
it tasted good—and we drank liquids
that also tasted good although
they were across the room and on the wall.
The phone rang. It was meaningless
like a proton, but Mother laughed
and said words that were exactly the words
she would have said, total illusion
and total reality at the same time, just as
Dad coughed fifty years later, it was me coughing,
which is why I left, heading east, and stopped
after fifteen hundred miles, and coughed again.
So this is Echo Lake? Sure looks nice.
Ice had once gone by.
High overhead was an iceberg just checking on things,
wings folded and in flames.
The soul materializes in the form of an echo and says
"I've been following you."

"But you are a shadow and only a shadow!"

"Only in the dark am I a shadow," the soul replies.

"In the light I am a very good lightbulb!"

"You are a big nothing something," the soul says.

The light changes and I start across.

Toothbrush

As the whisk broom
is the child of the ordinary broom,
which is cousin to the janitor's broom,
I am a toothbrush
when it comes to bristling,
insufficiently angry
or maybe too angry
to keep my bristles intact
since I know the debris
of the world is too great
for me to handle.
If I could save the world
by being crucified
I certainly would.
But who would nail
a toothbrush to a cross?

There Was a Man of Thessaly

There was a man of Thessaly
who jumped into a bush

and why, may I ask?
Because he was afraid of something?

Because he saw a bush and told himself
"I will jump into that bush"?

Maybe the fact that he had the idea
of jumping into the bush frightened him.

From great heights I have looked down
and thought "What if I went crazy for a moment

and found myself plummeting?" and stepped
back to remember who I am. I am

a man of Tulsa who jumps into his car
and by a miracle ends up somewhere else,

then jumps into the miracle and ends up
what?

History Lesson

I think that Geoffrey Chaucer did not move
the way a modern person moves.
He moved only an inch at a time, in what
we call stop action. Everyone in his day moved
like that, so they could be shot into a tapestry,
but also because time moved in short lurches
and was slightly jagged and had fewer colors
for them to be in. But that was good. Humanity
has to take it one step at a time.

The Question Bus

What about your friend? Will he shoot flames from his nostrils as he hurls you across the lawn? Or will he fall on his knees and adopt you as his one and only god? Somewhere in between.

Somewhere in between a rock and a click, where the abstractions roam about in their ghostly attire. They are haunting our thoughts, we who wear human attire. When they ask you to dance, you should refuse.

You should also refuse to pay the check when having dinner with sunlight: it's evening, and he should be in bed! He might not even be sunlight!

He might not even be a ghost. He may be the one you have grown weary of waiting for, the last one off the bus at the end of the line. He may be the bus itself, belching flames as all four tires explode. Is he really your friend?

The Nail

Just sitting here,
relaxing,
stretched out,
dead as
a nail
bent over
and smashed
into the grain
of a door
carted off to
the dump
some years
ago, you
get sleepier
and sleepier at
the thought
of that nail,
buried in wood,
with no lips
to tell the tale.

Mir

—There is no synonym for synonym

In the shtetl,
only the crowing
of two cocks
that sound alike.

I bang into the water pail,
blue in the morning light,
though to tell the truth
I am blue in any light,

a powdery royal blue.
Our village does not fly
through the air—it is
nailed to the ground

and we hold on for dear life—
to each other, to the trees,
the cottage doors, whatever,
and we sing our local ditty:

O the cats and the wellsprings!
O the dogs and the birdbath!
O! O! O!

Why I Would Like to Have Been
a Twelfth-Century Christian

I see
in my mind's eye
the crush of the faithful,
shoving jammed
into the basilica
of St. Denis
so tightly
they were
according to Suger
immobile
"as marble statues,"
some of them
screaming
while others
burst into riot,
and the priests
jumped
through a window
and ran away
with the holy relics.

For Morris Golde

It might have been when
I was standing in front of
Kierkegaard's grave thinking
that his name means
churchyard that Morris
Golde was breathing his
last in St. Vincent's, where
Jimmy died too, and what
was I doing then—and
what am I doing now?
Death throws everything
into high relief, itself
the highest—its uppermost
crag is where we sigh,
relax, and stretch out as
far as the mind can go.
I'm partway there is
a "deep" thought I can do
without, though I just
had it. I wish it would
get lighter faster. If it
were two weeks ago it
would be bright outside
instead of blue-gray.
Morris, you old thing.

Now at the Sahara

Where are those books I ordered and what
were they, oh yes, the *Divine Comedy* in three volumes
which I keep telling myself I am going to read
in toto, although I wonder about the "divine" part
that Dante himself didn't even have in his title
and to us "comedy" sounds like Shecky Greene
at the Sahara, Shecky who was funny and actually
kind of sad though not tragic. What is tragic is
that I started out thinking about Dante and
ended up thinking about Shecky Greene!

How to Be Perfect

Everything is perfect, dear friend.

— Kerouac

Get some sleep.

Don't give advice.

Take care of your teeth and gums.

Don't be afraid of anything beyond your control. Don't be afraid, for instance, that the building will collapse as you sleep, or that someone you love will suddenly drop dead.

Eat an orange every morning.

Be friendly. It will help make you happy.

Raise your pulse rate to 120 beats per minute for 20 straight minutes four or five times a week doing anything you enjoy.

Hope for everything. Expect nothing.

Take care of things close to home first. Straighten up your room before you save the world. Then save the world.

Know that the desire to be perfect is probably the veiled
expression of another desire—to be loved, perhaps, or not to die.

Make eye contact with a tree.

Be skeptical about all opinions, but try to see some value in each
of them.

Dress in a way that pleases both you and those around you.

Do not speak quickly.

Learn something every day. (*Dzien dobre!*)

Be nice to people before they have a chance to behave badly.

Don't stay angry about anything for more than a week, but don't
forget what made you angry. Hold your anger out at arm's length
and look at it, as if it were a glass ball. Then add it to your glass
ball collection.

Be loyal.

Wear comfortable shoes.

Design your activities so that they show a pleasing balance
and variety.

Be kind to old people, even when they are obnoxious. When you become old, be kind to young people. Do not throw your cane at them when they call you grandpa. They are your grandchildren!

Live with an animal.

Do not spend too much time with large groups of people.

If you need help, ask for it.

Cultivate good posture until it becomes natural.

If someone murders your child, get a shotgun and blow his head off.

Plan your day so you never have to rush.

Show your appreciation to people who do things for you, even if you have paid them, even if they do favors you don't want.

Do not waste money you could be giving to those who need it.

Expect society to be defective. Then weep when you find that it is far more defective than you imagined.

When you borrow something, return it in an even better condition.

As much as possible, use wooden objects instead of plastic or metal ones.

Look at that bird over there.

After dinner, wash the dishes.

Calm down.

Visit foreign countries, except those whose inhabitants have expressed a desire to kill you.

Don't expect your children to love you, so they can, if they want to.

Meditate on the spiritual. Then go a little further, if you feel like it. What is out (in) there?

Sing, every once in a while.

Be on time, but if you are late do not give a detailed and lengthy excuse.

Don't be too self-critical or too self-congratulatory.

Don't think that progress exists. It doesn't.

Walk upstairs.

Do not practice cannibalism.

Imagine what you would like to see happen, and then don't do anything to make it impossible.

Take your phone off the hook at least twice a week.

Keep your windows clean.

Extirpate all traces of personal ambitiousness.

Don't use the word *extirpate* too often.

Forgive your country every once in a while. If that is not possible, go to another one.

If you feel tired, rest.

Grow something.

Do not wander through train stations muttering, "We're all going to die!"

Count among your true friends people of various stations of life.

Appreciate simple pleasures, such as the pleasure of chewing, the pleasure of warm water running down your back, the pleasure of a cool breeze, the pleasure of falling asleep.

Do not exclaim, "Isn't technology wonderful!"

Learn how to stretch your muscles. Stretch them every day.

Don't be depressed about growing older. It will make you feel even older. Which is depressing.

Do one thing at a time.

If you burn your finger, put ice on it immediately. If you bang your finger with a hammer, hold your hand in the air for twenty minutes. You will be surprised by the curative powers of ice and gravity.

Learn how to whistle at ear-splitting volume.

Be calm in a crisis. The more critical the situation, the calmer you should be.

Enjoy sex, but don't become obsessed with it. Except for brief periods in your adolescence, youth, middle age, and old age.

Contemplate everything's opposite.

If you're struck with the fear that you've swum out too far in the ocean, turn around and go back to the lifeboat.

Keep your childish self alive.

Answer letters promptly. Use attractive stamps, like the one with a tornado on it.

Cry every once in a while, but only when alone. Then appreciate how much better you feel. Don't be embarrassed about feeling better.

Do not inhale smoke.

Take a deep breath.

Do not smart off to a policeman.

Do not step off the curb until you can walk all the way across the street. From the curb you can study the pedestrians who are trapped in the middle of the crazed and roaring traffic.

Be good.

Walk down different streets.

Backwards.

Remember beauty, which exists, and truth, which does not. Notice that the idea of truth is just as powerful as the idea of beauty.

Stay out of jail.

In later life, become a mystic.

Use Colgate toothpaste in the new Tartar Control formula.

Visit friends and acquaintances in the hospital. When you feel it is time to leave, do so.

Be honest with yourself, diplomatic with others.

Do not go crazy a lot. It's a waste of time.

Read and reread great books.

Dig a hole with a shovel.

In winter, before you go to bed, humidify your bedroom.

Know that the only perfect things are a 300 game in bowling and a 27-batter, 27-out game in baseball.

Drink plenty of water. When asked what you would like to drink, say, "Water, please."

Ask "Where is the loo?" but not "Where can I urinate?"

Be kind to physical objects.

Beginning at age forty, get a complete "physical" every few years from a doctor you trust and feel comfortable with.

Don't read the newspaper more than once a year.

Learn how to say "hello," "thank you," and "chopsticks"
in Mandarin.

Belch and fart, but quietly.

Be especially cordial to foreigners.

See shadow puppet plays and imagine that you are one of the
characters. Or all of them.

Take out the trash.

Love life.

Use exact change.

When there's shooting in the street, don't go near the window.

Sea Chantey

Hello, sailor.
I hear you are sailing
on a craft across
the water, crossing
the big blue liquid
that is green and gray
and sometimes boiling
with lobsters and
other seafood that
roaring-with-laughter
King Neptune sends
swirling up through
vertical currents in
his ocean domain, at
the bottom of which
he sits on a seashell
throne, holding a small
goat on his face most
unpleasantly! So when
you go floating across
the briny deep, never
visit the bottom,
even if you have bubbles
and rubber tubes and plenty
of life inside your body.
Remember that goat.

Downstairs

In Edwardian England the women's knickers
were slit all the way up the inside of the thigh

for convenience in the loo, given the corset
and layers of other bindings that held

the body in place, but also for easy access
when a randy fellow would no longer be able

to control the bulge inside his trousers
and you were alone with him in the pantry

while the male servants were asleep, or
so you thought, for some could hear the clatter

of pots and pans as he pushed you against the wall
and the glaze in his eyes shot you a delicious panic.

Nails

How did people trim their toenails in ancient times?
The Virgin Mary's toenails look fine
in the paintings of the Italian Renaissance,
and it's a good thing too, for it would be hard
to worship a figure with very long toenails.
Perugino scoffed at a religion aimed
toward God but whose real attention
was on Mary, but he gave her nice toenails.
I've never looked at Jesus' toenails, even
though they're near the holes
in his feet, where the other nails were.
Cruelty is so graphic and hard to understand,
whereas beauty, even the beauty of a toe,
makes perfect sense. To me, anyway.

It Is Almost Unbearable

that people are so different from us
whenever we lift the veil

on which lilacs are shifting
and their eyes are still there

among the gyrations and flattened
slantings of their spirits, as if

spiraling upward through time
until they hit us and our cups

runneth over, though clear
is the liquid and bitter its taste

to our narrow tongues. And
we rejoice for only a moment

and joke for the eternity in which
we know we will never dart about

happily, for the veil we lift is
our own skin, a tarp in wind.

Country Room

You are in a room
in the country
in a country
that has plenty of room

to walk around
in.
You walk to one
end of the room,

turn and walk
out the door
into the room next
to the door

that leads out
to the country
side and to
everywhere

so you turn
around and go
back in to
where you were.

But now the room
has advanced
in time ahead
of you and you

will have to hurry
up or else
the room will leave
you far behind.

Jeopardy

Sometimes when I phoned
my mother back in Tulsa, she would
say, "Hold on a minute, Ron, let me
turn this thing down," the thing
her TV, and she would look
around for the remote and then fumble
with its little buttons as an irritation
mounted in me and an impatience
and I felt like blurting out "You watch TV
too much and it's too loud and why
don't you go outside" because I was
unable to face my dread of her aging
and my heart made cold toward her
by loving her though not wanting to give up
my life and live near her so she
could see me every day and not
just hear me, which is why she
turned the TV down and said,
"Okay, that's better," then sometimes
launched into a detailed account
of whatever awful show she was watching.

Sitting Down Somewhere Else

I look out the window and the first thing I see
is a large, immobile god (a tree).

The house is surrounded by such gods
whose heads, like mine, are in the clouds

that have come far down to drift and be vague
the way they were that first night in The Hague

when I sat alone in a Chinese restaurant
whose waiter didn't ask What would you like

and I heard the owners a few tables away
repeat the words the language records had them say:

Hello! How are you? I am fine.
Is this a good place for me to dine?

The emptiness of the room was worse
than the emptiness of the universe

and I had nowhere else to go but here,
which is where I think I am, or was, or there.

The Art of the Sonnet

Last night I said hello
to the little muse
the smaller than usual muse

She was floating toward me
a plaster figurine
on a cloud

but her plaster lips
could not return my greeting.
That's the first part

and in Japan.
Now the figurine
drifts past and turns

a smile erasing
her face

The Alpinist

I have a body without a head
and a head without a body
If only I could get them affixed
to one another
but the head cannot walk
and the body cannot know
that the head exists
so I must hover between the two
like whatever it is
that links the two parts of a simile

The simile, however, is unhappy
lying there all by itself, it wants
to be part of a sentence, preferably one
without other similes crowding in
like sheep

Next to the sheep is a river
you never noticed, for you saw
the one that was there yesterday
and the one the day before that
which was also never

I am climbing I think it's a ladder
but I don't have to hold on

I don't even have to climb
I just do
Or it's something akin to climbing
on something akin to a ladder

From up here I can see both my head
and my body and the river between
and when the river stops flowing
I will find myself next to a hut in the Alps
with cows and flowers but without words

But that's for later

Gothic Red

That is a very beautiful growl you have,
great-grandpa, but it is scaring me a little.
If you would please ask great-grandma
to growl a little too, it would help.
You could even harmonize your growls
so they could hang from your faces
in complementary colors and not just
black and white, and your eyes, glazed
with what we used to think of as age,
could close slowly and then stay that way,
for a while, anyway, for the wind
is coming up the lane and into the window
to enlarge you to sky size not
for the sake of your so-called immortality
but so you can growl even louder
in the sleep that has become both yours and ours.

Charlie Chan Wins Again

Now honorable leg broken.
The fog drifts over the docks.
It is a terrible movie
I can't watch, but I do.
Charlie goes into the next room
and removes his hat: ladies.
They fuss and fret, but Charlie
shows them his broken leg
and receives honorable sympathy.
His son dashes in: Dad,
come quick! Charlie tells ladies:
Do not leave room please.
Their fluttering flustered looks
bounce off the walls, which
change from medium gray
to pulsating red. Charlie peeps
in door, says, Red good luck.

Thinking about the Moon

As a child I thought the moon
existed only at night:

there it was
in the dark sky.

When I saw it in daytime
I knew it was the moon

but it wasn't the real one.
It was that other one.

The real moon had moonlight,
silver and blue

And the full moon was so big
it seemed close, but

to what? (I didn't know
I was on Earth.)

This for That

What will I have for breakfast?
I wish I had some plums
like the ones in Williams's poem.
He apologized to his wife
for eating them
but what he did not
do was apologize to those
who would read his poem
and also not be able to eat them.
That is why I like his poem
when I am not hungry.
Right now I do not like him
or his poem. This is just
to say that.

Nelly

Nelly was a girl I once knew in Brooklyn.
She was a nice girl, a bit on the heavy side,
but generous and with an easy laugh
when you tried to kiss her, which was pretty much
every minute you were with her, though
it was all in fun, there was no question
of the thing actually getting "serious,"
though when you lay in bed sweating
through the summer nights, you turned
your head toward the window and thought
about maybe she was the girl for you.

Very Post-Impressionism

The trouble with listening to this music
is that it turns you into a lily pad
on a small pond on a rural property
not far from Paris, and sitting on you
is a large frog named Claude Monet.
You want to strangle him, not
for his paintings, but for the fact that
he doesn't know you're there.
He thinks you are only a lily pad,
and you know that when the music stops
you will be a person again, but
by then he will be dead and gone,
beyond the reach of your fingers.

The Absolutely Huge and Incredible
Injustice in the World

What makes us so mean?
We are meaner than gorillas,
the ones we like to blame our genetic aggression on.
It is in our nature to hide behind what Darwin said about
    survival,
as if survival were the most important thing on earth.
It isn't.
You know—surely it has occurred to you—
that there is no way that humankind will survive
another million years. We'll be lucky to be around
another five hundred. Why?
Because we are so mean
that we would rather kill everyone and everything on earth
than let anybody get the better of us:
"Give me liberty or give me death!"
Why didn't he just say "Grrr, let's kill each other!"?

A nosegay of pansies leans toward us in a glass of water
on a white tablecloth bright in the sunlight
at the ocean where children are frolicking,
then looking around and wondering—
about what we cannot say, for we are imagining
how we would kill the disgusting man and woman
at the next table. Tonight we could throw an electrical storm
into their bed. No more would they spit on the veranda!

Actually they aren't that bad, it's just
that I am talking mean in order to be more
like my fellow humans—it's lonely feeling like a saint,
which I do one second every five weeks,
but that one second is so intense I can't stand up
and then I figure out that it's ersatz, I can't be a saint,
I am not even a religious person, I am hardly a person at all
except when I look at you and think
that this life with you must go on forever
because it is so perfect, with all its imperfections,
like your waistline that exists a little too much,
like my hairline that doesn't exist at all!
Which means that my bald head feels good
on your soft round belly that feels good too.
If only everyone were us!

But sometimes we are everyone, we get mad
at the world and mean as all get-out,
which means we want to tell the world to get out
of this, our world. Who are all these awful people?
Why, it's your own grandma, who was so nice to you—
you mistook her for someone else. She actually was
someone else, but you had no way of knowing that,
just as you had no way of knowing that the taxi driver
saves his pennies all year
to go to Paris for Racine at the Comédie Française.
Now he is reciting a long speech in French from *Andromache*
and you arrive at the corner of This and That

and though Andromache's noble husband Hector has been killed
and his corpse has been dragged around the walls of Troy by an
    unusually mean Achilles,
although she is forced into slavery and a marriage
to save the life of her son, and then people around her
get killed, commit suicide, and go crazy, the driver is in paradise,
he has taken you back to his very mean teacher
in the unhappy school in Port-au-Prince and then
to Paris and back to the French language of the seventeenth century
and then to ancient Greece and then to the corner of This and That.
Only a mean world would have this man driving around in a city
where for no reason someone is going to fire a bullet into the
    back of his head!

It was an act of kindness
on the part of the person who placed both numbers and letters
on the dial of the phone so we could call WAverly,
ATwater, CAnareggio, BLenheim, and MAdison,
DUnbar and OCean, little worlds in themselves
we drift into as we dial, and an act of cruelty
to change everything into numbers only, not just phone numbers
that get longer and longer, but statistical analysis,
cost averaging, collateral damage, death by peanut,
inflation rates, personal identification numbers, access codes,
and the whole raving Raft of the Medusa
that drives out any thought of pleasantness
until you dial 1-800-MATTRES and in no time get a mattress
that is complete and comfy and almost under you,

even though you didn't need one! The men
come in and say Here's the mattress where's
the bedroom? And the bedroom realizes it can't run away.
You can't say that the people who invented the bedroom
        were mean,
only a bedroom could say that, if it could say anything.
It's a good thing that bedrooms can't talk!
They might keep you up all night telling you things
you don't want to know. "Many years ago,
in this very room . . ." Eeek, shut up! I mean,
please don't tell me anything, I'm sorry I shouted at you.
And the walls subside into their somewhat foreverness.
The wrecking ball will mash its grimace into the plaster and oof,
down they will come, lathe and layers of personal history,
but the ball is not mean, nor is the man who pulls the handle
that directs the ball on its pendulous course, but another man
—and now a woman strides into his office and slaps his face
        hard—
the man whose bottom line is changing its color
wants to change it back. So good-bye, building
where we made love, laughed, wept, ate, and watched TV
all at the same time! Where our dog waited by the door,
eyes fixed on the knob, where a runaway stream came whooshing
down the hallway, where I once expanded to fill the whole room
and then deflated, just to see what it would feel like,
where on Saturday mornings my infant son stood by the bedside
and sang, quietly, "Wa-a-a-ke up" to his snoozing parents.
I can never leave all the kindness I have felt in this apartment,

but if a big black iron wrecking ball comes flying toward me,
zoop, out I go! For there must be
kindness somewhere else in the world,
maybe even out of it, though I'm not crazy
about the emptiness of outer space. I have to live
here, with finite life and inner space and with
the horrible desire to love everything and be disappointed
the way my mother was until that moment
when she rolled her eyes toward me as best she could
and squeezed my hand when I asked, "Do you know who I am?"
then let go of life.

The other question was, Did I know who I was?

It is hard not to be appalled by existence.
The pointlessness of matter turns us into cornered animals
that otherwise are placid or indifferent,
we hiss and bare our fangs and attack.
But how many people have felt the terror of existence?
Was Genghis Khan horrified that he and everything else existed?
Was Hitler or Pol Pot?
Or any of the other charming figures of history?
Je le doute.
It was something else made them mean.
Something else made Napoleon think it glorious
to cover the frozen earth with a hundred thousand bloody corpses.
Something else made . . . oh, name your monster
and his penchant for destruction,

name your own period in history when a darkness swept over us
and made not existing seem like the better choice,
as if the solution to hunger were to hurl oneself
into a vat of boiling radioactive carrots!

Life is so awful!
I hope that lion tears me to pieces!
It is good that those men wearing black hoods
are going to strip off my skin and force me
to gape at my own intestines spilling down onto the floor!
Please drive spikes through not only my hands and feet
but through my eyes as well!
For this world is to be fled as soon as possible
via the purification of martyrdom.
This from the God of Christian Love.
Cupid hovers overhead, perplexed.
Long ago Zeus said he was tired
and went to bed: if you're not going to exist
it's best to be asleep.
The Christian God is like a cranky two-thousand-year-old baby
whose fatigue delivers him into an endless tantrum.
he will never grow up
because you can't grow up unless people listen to you,
and they can't listen because they are too busy being mean
or fearing the meanness of others.
How can I blame them?
I too am afraid. I can be jolted by an extremely violent movie,
but what is really scary is that someone *wanted* to make the film!

He is only a step away from the father
who took his eight-year-old daughter and her friend to the park
and beat and stabbed them to death. Uh-oh.
"He seemed like a normal guy," said his neighbor, Thelma,
who refused to divulge her last name to reporters.
She seemed like a normal gal, just as the reporters seemed like
    normal vampires.
In some cultures it is normal to eat bugs or people
or to smear placenta on your face at night, to buy
a car whose price would feed a village for thirty years,
to waste your life and, while you're at it, waste everyone
    else's too!
Hello, America. It is dawn,
wake up and smell yourselves.
You smell normal.

My father was not normal,
he was a criminal, a scuffler, a tough guy,
and though he did bad things
he was never mean.
He didn't like mean people, either.
Sometimes he would beat them up
or chop up their shoes!
I have never beaten anyone up,
but it might be fun to chop up some shoes.
Would you please hand me that cleaver, Thelma?

But Thelma is insulted by my request,
even though I said *please*, because she has the face of a cleaver

that flies through the air toward me and lodges
in my forehead. "Get it yourself,
lughead!" she spits, then twenty years later
she changes *lughead* to *fuckhead*.
I change my name to Jughead
and go into the poetry protection program
so my poems can go out and live under assumed names
in Utah and Muskogee.

Anna Chukhno looks up and sees me
through her violet Ukrainian eyes
and says Good morning most pleasantly inflected. Oh
to ride in a horse-drawn carriage with her at midnight
down the wide avenues of Kiev and erase
the ditch at Babi Yar from human history!
She looks up and asks How would you like that?
I say In twenties and she counts them out
as if the air around her were not shattered by her beauty
and my body thus divided into zones:
hands the place of metaphysics, shins the area of moo,
bones the cost of living, and so on.
Is it cruel that I cannot cover her with kisses?
No, it is beautiful that I cannot cover her with kisses,
it is better that I walk out into the sunlight
with the blessing of having spoken with an actual goddess
who gave me four hundred dollars!
And I am reassembled
as my car goes forward

into the oncoming rays of aggression
that bounce off my glasses and then
start penetrating, and soon my eyes
turn into abandoned coal mines
whose canaries explode into an evil song
that echoes exactly nowhere.

At least I am not in Rwanda in 1994 or The Sudan in '05
or Guantanamo or The Tombs, or in a ditch outside Rio,
clubbed to death and mutilated. No Cossack
bears down on me with sword raised and gleaming
at my Jewish neck and no time for me
to cry out "It is only my neck that is Jewish!
The rest is Russian Orthodox!" No smiling man tips back
his hat and says to his buddies, "Let's teach
this nigguh a lesson." I don't need a lesson, sir,
I am Ethiopian, this is my first time in your country!
But you gentlemen are joking . . .

Prepare my cave and then kindly forget where it was.
A crust of bread will suffice and a stream nearby,
the chill of evening filtering in with the blind god
who *is* the chill of evening and who touches us
though we can't raise our hands to stroke his misty beard
    in which
two hundred million stars have wink and glimmer needles.

I had better go back to the bank, we have
only three hundred and eighty-five dollars left.
Those fifteen units of beauty went fast.

As does everything.
But meanness comes back right away
while kindness takes its own sweet time
and compassion is busy shimmering always a little above us and
    behind,
swooping down and transfusing us only when we don't expect it
and then only for a moment.
How can I trap it?
Allow it in and then
turn my body into steel? No.
The exit holes will still be there and besides
compassion doesn't need an exit it is an exit—
from the prison that each moment is,
and just as each moment replaces the one before it
each jolt of meanness replaces the one before it
and pretty soon you get to like those jolts,
you and millions of other dolts who like to be electrocuted
by their own feelings. The hippopotamus
sits on you with no sense of pleasure, he doesn't
even know you are there, any more than he takes notice
of the little white bird atop his head, and when
he sees you flattened against the ground
he doesn't even think Uh-oh he just trots away
with the bird still up there looking around.

Saint Augustine stole the apples from his neighbor's tree
and didn't apologize for thirty years, by which time
his neighbor was probably dead and in no mood
for apologies. Augustine's mother became a saint
and then a city in California—Santa Monica,
where everything exists so it can be driven past,
except the hippopotamus that stands on the freeway
in the early dawn and yawns into your high beams.
"Hello," he seems to grunt, "I can't be your friend
and I can't be your enemy, I am like compassion,
I go on just beyond you, no matter how many times
you crash into me and die because you never learned
to crash and live." Then he ambles away.
Could Saint Augustine have put on that much weight?
I thought compassion makes you light
or at least have light, the way it has light around it
in paintings, like the one of the screwdriver
that appeared just when the screw was coming loose
from the wing of the airplane in which Santa Monica was riding
    into heaven,
smiling as if she had just imagined how to smile
the first smile of any saint, a promise toward the perfection
of everything that is and isn't.

Afternoon

Who is here with me?
My mother who is an Indian.
(I am not an Indian.)
She is sweeping the teepee
with a broom of sticks
as if to cover her tracks.
(She has no tracks she
is so light.)
I have come through
the air as a drawing
on a piece of paper
to tell her that she
is not an Indian,
but the sound
of the sweeping drowns
out my crinkling voice
and an updraft lifts
me up and out
over the village
that seems to sail away.
(It is so light.)

All in White

All in white my love went riding—
is that a misquotation? and if so
of whom? It's the kind of line
that Ted loved back in 1960
because of its lilt and in his mind
a kind of Irishness. Kenneth
Patchen? What did I see in him
that I don't now and still want to?
A dark lilt and a slide through pain,
both of which I wanted and didn't have
—I had a light lilt and moderate pain.
Ted had a dark and light lilt and
was fleeing from pain. I said
"I don't have any pain." Ted said
"Yes you do ha ha!" The springtime
was lovely and out there all
in white my love went riding.

Dead or Alive in Belgium

Somebody you think is dead is alive
and somebody you think is alive is dead

Sometimes it comes as a happy surprise
and sometimes you wonder

She was given a few days, hours perhaps
Now she looks stronger and even prettier

His chances of surviving were so-so
Now he's going to Belgium

which takes strength, just the thought
—Why do I say such things?

Because there's a Frenchman inside me
who jumps out every once in a while

Bonjour! Voilà, un bon café bien chaud!
Then he forgets to jump out

Or I jump out in front of him
I am much bigger than he is

He does not want to go to Belgium
or even say anything nice about Belgium

I don't want to go to Belgium
though I would like to go to Bruges

Ghent Antwerp and Brussels
and go inside the paintings there

and stand next to the Virgin
her forehead so large and pure

and be there alive with her again
oil on board in Belgium

Whiz and Bang

You hammer away on
the hills and braes of
bonny Scotland, where
oh the thrill of the thought
of it the heather
runs up like a girl all fresh
and wind-blown to shake
her head and wag a
finger at your naughty
naughty thoughts,
about her, of
course, and you
hammer those hills and braes
with all your might.

Standoff with Frosty

Every time I sit down to do some serious work
my stomach tells me it's time to go downstairs
and see what's in the fridge, but when
I reach in there an icy hand
grabs my wrist and thrusts me away
from the territory of the snowman.
Yes, Frosty himself.
He lives in there with a banjo and a carrot.
He plays the banjo and thinks about the carrot,
but it is a dull existence, and he is disgruntled.
How can I make him happy? There is no way,
for he can neither hear nor understand my words.
I cannot reason with him, describe the arctic nights
that gave him "life," nor lure his melancholy world
away from him. He is stuck and so am I.

A Train for Kenneth

One train may hide another
or it might hide the mountain
into which it disappears and
hides itself. You step
into that tunnel, stop,
the tracks gleaming at your feet
but no light further on.

(This is not a metaphor.)
(So what is it?)

It's a stanza, in which
the train is hiding. You
can't see it because
the letters are so dark—
the light around them
makes them even darker.

But now the train comes
out the other end and smoke
is trailing from its stack, for
this happened in olden days,
when chugging existed.

In Memoriam K.

So what will you do tomorrow
now that he has died today?
Why, you'll get dressed and
fix your breakfast as you always do,
then make some coffee for your wife
and bring it to her bed, where she will say
Thank you—the nicest moment of the day,
for me, anyway. And then the sunlight
on the lawn, song in feathers
high in a tree and hidden,
as if their notes were sung
inside my head which is
come to think of it where
I hear them, as I hear him,
he who made me so much
who I am and now must be alone
with him now he is gone.

The Goldberg Variations

When I heard Glenn Gould talking
on the radio today—his voice from long ago—
I knew no matter how eccentric how
difficult how crabby he might have been
I knew I'd trust whatever he had to say
and I did, so well-structured his sentences
were, and precise his words,
and for a moment
I felt regret I never knew him though
I don't think I could have talked all night
on the phone with him but then
maybe I would have especially when
I was young enough to kill myself for art.

Mad Scientist

Up goes the mad scientist to the room in his tower
where his instruments gleam in the half-light
while his thoughts are surrounded by the half-dark
that filters out from his heart, but when he goes in
and looks around, all he can see is the chair
covered with a bright red and green serape
and sparks are fizzing in the thought balloon
above his head, for yes, he is a cartoon scientist,
just as everything I think about is a cartoon something
because anything cartoon is immortal
in its own funny little way.

Hound Dog

"You ain't nothin' but a hound dog"
sounds like an insult and if it were directed
to a person yes I would say it is an insult
but if it were directed to a dog I would say
that it is not an insult, it is simply a statement
of fact, like telling a rock that it is a rock,
though of course since a rock cannot hear the words
it would make less sense to speak to it, whereas
a hound dog could not only hear but in its own
dog way understand the feeling of the statement
via its tone and some other method dogs have
of knowing things. For instance the hound dog
would know that if you said such a thing you
would be either a rather daffy ontologist or a shit,
but either way you would fall over sideways if
the dog were to answer back, "You ain't nothin'
but an ontologist" or "a shit." Fortunately for you
the hound dog says nothing. It rolls its supposedly sad
eyes up to yours and just looks at you, and whether
you are an ontologist or a shit it makes no difference.
You ain't nothin'.

Fantasy Block

I would like to have a sexual fantasy
about the young girl I see in the gym,
the one who undulates up and down
on an aerobic machine revealing
the smooth skin of her lower back
as it swells out toward her hips,
her hair pulled up in back
with a tortoiseshell clasp
and a misty blush spreading
from her high cheekbones back
to her ears in each of which
a small silver ring is glittering,
but I can't think of anything.

Words from the Front

We don't look as young
as we used to
except in dim light
especially in
the soft warmth of candlelight
when we say
in all sincerity
You're so cute
and
You're my cutie.
Imagine
two old people
behaving like this.
It's enough
to make you happy.

Pikakirjoitusvihko

I hold the door open for a frail, elderly woman.

•

She looks surprised.

•

I will never recover from having a mental flash of Jimmy Durante
the moment I learned that Dante's real name was Durante.

•

The more our public officials talk about integrity, the deeper
burns their hypocrisy. (Thinking up such a truism makes me
feel contaminated.)

•

The French have a reputation for verbal exactitude, so why do
they call a tuxedo a "smoking"?

•

When I first looked in the mirror, I had always been there.

•

Waiting for the light to change, a nice-looking young man in his twenties unwraps a candy bar and drops the wrapper a few feet from the trash basket.

•

The American economic system—if anything so out of control can be called a system—requires ever more production and consumption, resulting in greater and greater destruction of the natural world and increasingly invasive attacks on the nervous system. This juggernaut knows how to go in one direction only. I am part of this system, being invested in it, mostly, I tell myself, to protect my wife from a future of penury. My first duty is to her, despite my mounting shame and disgust at the ruin that we, especially in the West, are wreaking upon the world. It's strange that these monumentally important—if obvious—ideas sometimes strike me as tedious, as if they were a minor annoyance.

•

She walks in and asks, "What are you doing?" when she means something else.

•

I have to call Ted Greenwald.

•

For a writer it's good to be angry all the time because then more people can like your work.

•

On the last day of a stay in a distant city, I try to remain
interested and busy, although I know I am just marking time
until the hour of departure: I stand in the Luxembourg Garden
but I am not fully there. Now I notice that I have begun to do
something similar in my life in general. On the verge of sixty, I
have started to mark time. Hey!

•

Fiddlesticks.

•

(A secret homage.)

•

We refer to the decades of a century as the twenties, thirties,
forties, etc.—even the teens—but why do I not know the name of
the first decade of a century? Is it a blind spot particular to me?

•

Fantasy and Fugue in A Minor.

•

"Morning ablutions" used to sound like something that people
did in the nineteenth century. Now *I* do them.

•

Differences of race, national origin, religion, social level, wealth, gender, age, political ideology, philosophy—all can be barriers to compassion. But what about intelligence? How many people of noticeably lower intelligence do you count among your true friends?

•

It's almost midnight. No wonder it's late.

•

I'm not sure what it means that when I learned to tie my own shoes, at the late age of six, I did so by myself, inventing a curious series of loops and moves that I still use, fifty-five years later.

•

When the footsteps in the hallway stop, a long shadow flows under the door. Then he moves on.

•

In movies about Indians there is never any evidence—in the teepees or elsewhere in the village—of a bathroom. So where did they . . . ?

•

Shop name in upper Manhattan: "Explosions 2000—Men, Women, & Children."

•

The miracle of existing and being able to say so and have drapes.

•

Farrago.

•

The day I was born, German saboteurs came ashore on the coast of Florida.

•

Title: "Whatever May Happen to Your Hair in a Song."

•

"By convention sweet, by convention bitter, by convention hot, by convention cold, by convention color: but in reality atoms and void." (Democritus, quoted by Sextus)

•

"One day, looking at a painting by Matisse, I lost my back." (Bernard Noël)

•

The origin of the word *turmoil* is unknown.

•

How many people, alone in the privacy of their own homes, have ever sung the national anthem? Probably very few. Maybe none! Solitude is not patriotic.

•

The fly
on the countertop
is not there

•

Buenos Aires, Argentina. At least 60,000 people attended an
outdoor Roman Catholic mass Monday to mourn the theft of
former President Juan Perón's hands.

•

"As a result of this luxation of our intellects the shameful
misconception of Marxism could be put about and even believed,
that economic forces and material interests determine the course
of the world. This grotesque over-estimation of the economic
factor was conditioned by our worship of technological progress,
which was itself the fruit of rationalism and utilitarianism after
they had killed the mysteries and acquitted man of guilt and sin.
But they had forgotten to free him of folly and myopia, and he
seemed only fit to mould the world after the pattern of his own
banality." (Jan Huizinga, *Homo Ludens)*

•

For the past thirty-five years I have been meaning to find and
read *The Heart of the Continent* by Fitz Hugh Ludlow, 1870,
wondering if it might be one of those "lost" classics, which I
seem to find more alluring than "found" ones.

•

"He has bought a Madonna by Andrea del Sarto for six hundred sequins." (Goethe, *Italian Journey*, translated by Mayer and Auden)

•

According to Oscar Wilde, women are sphinxes without secrets. Does he mean that they are simply colossal statues? If so, he is right.

•

(Just kidding.)

•

"No man who is in a hurry is quite civilized." (Will Durant) Is this one way that technology is taking us to new forms of savagery?

•

Some things everyone should know:
1) How to swim
2) How to administer cardio-pulmonary resuscitation and the Heimlich maneuver
3) How to whistle loudly
4) How to treat kitchen burns and banged parts of the body by immediately applying ice or cold water

•

I must go back to the Louvre to see an intensely erotic and silly painting called *Aurora and Cephalus*.

•

It's irritating to be almost old without having grown up.

•

A sudden whim to drive 300 miles to Vermont and get new tires.

•

Hearing that Wittgenstein came from the wealthiest family in Austria has made me—for the moment, at least—less excited about his ideas. What does that say about me?

•

You are dying for lunch, so you heat up the soup. But now it is too hot to eat.

•

My guilt at not wanting to be buried in Tulsa—as if I were abandoning my mother for eternity.

•

Looking up *Pyrrhic victory* in the dictionary isn't worth the trouble.

•

What to do while a democracy votes itself out of existence?

•

When asked what he wanted done with his body after his death, Philip Whalen said, "Have them lay me out on a bed of frozen raspberries."

•

A sound enters the room like a cardboard box the size of the room entering the room.

•

An hour ago I was going to write, "My life hasn't been what it might have been, because I haven't saved the world from unhappiness, rapacity, destruction, fear, and hate," but the phone rang, and when I finally returned to the blank page, I stared at it with no idea of why it was there waiting for me. Then: "Ah, evil!"

•

On some level, things don't get better or worse, they just *get*. That I don't know what this means is an example.

•

Whether civilization wants to admit it or not, at this very moment all over the world little girls are masturbating.

•

This notebook, I think I bought it in Kiev. I had gone swimming in the Dnieper, mainly because I liked the idea that one day I would be able to tell myself that I had once swam in a river whose name begins with *D-n*—forgetting that the recent and nearby nuclear power plant disaster at Chernobyl might have rendered the water highly radioactive!

•

Courtesy is more efficient than the lack of it.

•

If I get a fatal disease, I am going to be very mad at it. I will blame it for my death.

•

The worth of that is that which it contains / And that is this, and this . . ." (Shakespeare, almost Gertrude Stein, *Sonnet 74*)

•

Does Euclidean geometry say that the angle of reflection is equal to the angle of incidence? If so, it can't be true. The angle of incidence must come first. But if we turn it around, the same problem arises. (Only by focusing on such ideas can I avoid raging at the way "things" are.)

•

Fyodor = Theodore. Therefore, Ted Dostoyevsky.

•

And, as the bombs fall in Baghdad tonight, how charming the melodrama of thunder outside my window.

•

Is it snobbery or nostalgia that makes me sad when I think of how it has been decades since I heard the two words that echoed throughout my adolescence: *intellectual curiosity*. And although one still hears the word *conformity*, it is no longer a pejorative term; now we are *on the same page, getting with the program, team players*.

•

If you live long enough and look hard enough, you will eventually—to your great relief and your great sorrow—find your humanity.

•

A French friend wrote to me, "C'est la fin des carottes" (It's the end of the carrots), but I don't know what it means. Maybe "That's all she wrote"? (I sent your saddle home.)

•

How could I have bought this notebook in Kiev when the word on its cover, *Pikakirjoitusvihko,* is, it turns out, Finnish?

To the Russian Poets

If I write poetry thirty minutes a decade,
that's enough! if I write very quickly

filling hundreds of pages with *If* and *Oops*
but with other, nobler words as well,

like *Poland* and *moustache, no job now,*
fall by the wayside, bone, and *finger, wisp,*

so that I emerge an Iron Country
Iron Man, poet whose jaw is stronger

than Mayakovsky's, whose imagery
is quicker than Pasternak's, heart

more broken than Akhmatova's and
whose shoes are whizzing more

than Khlebnikov's with their waving yellow laces.
Slavic poets of the great undertow,

you can smile now, it's snowing and cold
and empty and you're hungry again, almost starving.

Construction

He was as stiff as a board
and as hard as nails

are not really similes,
they are clichés,

which means we hear them
as single units whose meaning

we already know, unless
we have never heard them before.

If we add
He was as big as a house

there appears the image of the man
using his own body and spirit

as building materials,
adding story upon story

until the architecture of the house
and the architecture of language

both collapse
like a ton of bricks.

Why God Did What He Did

God hates you
which is why he created the world
and put you in it
and gave you the power to realize
that you're here
for a while
and then poof

and while you're here
you come to see
that the world too will be destroyed
by a fiery bowling ball,
ten thousand times the size of the earth,
hurtling through space
at this very moment

so that nothing absolutely nothing
means anything
because that's what God wants
and he wants you to know it
because he really hates you
and he wants you to know that too

The Idea of Being Hurled at Key West

What if she, in her magnificence,
picked you up and held you high aloft
in a glittering instant, then, with
a grunt, threw you down the beach
two hundred yards, to where
the stars are now both in the sky
and circling round your head as she
comes loping down the long decline
to pick you up and hurl you once again?

Judy Holliday

Don't think of saying a word about it I
will kill you positively and I'm not kidding,
mmm mmm mmm. The Romans
did not brook interference. They
liked water and plenty of it, it was all
around them, they had toys too,
so why not? Why not what? Why not
anything? I mean if you like water that much
you may as well like everything and
lots more and they did, up to a point, then
they were a dud. The barbarians
made them be a dud. But up
they arose in handmade robes and sang
and curls appeared, on rocks and air,
and before you knew it, boom,
they were back in business.

Method

Sometimes Kenneth Koch's method I guess you'd call it
was to have a general notion of the whole poem
before he started
such as the history of jazz or the boiling point of water
or talking to things that can't talk back
(as he put it) that is apostrophes
whereas my method I guess I'd call it
is to start and go
wherever the poem seems to lead

Sometimes it doesn't lead anywhere
other than to a dead end, and when I turn around
the street has disappeared and I find myself
sitting in a room.
Sometimes it leads somewhere
I have no interest in being
or the way I get there is contrived or silly

I have a face
that stays mostly on the front of my head
while inside my head wheels
are turning with a sound like music heard across water
over which a breeze rises and falls
cooling my face.
I should be nicer to my face

send it on vacation or just let it go relax
over there under that shady maple
Instead I let it carry all kinds of packages
back and forth from my brain to the world
though of course my brain is a part of the world
I should send my brain on vacation too
though it tells me now that I should consider the possibility that
    it has always been on vacation
Tricky brain! in which
the personality skates around
and the moral character rises and sits, rises and sits
and whose doorway at the bottom has a sign
that says . . . there's not enough light to read it.
I wish there were.

Kenneth said Write a poem in which each line begins with
"I wish . . ."
I wish gorilla
I wish squish
I wish *deux-tiers*
I wish onrushing cloudburst
and the hundred thousand one-second-old wishes came
    pouring forth
and still are pouring forth
like babies in trees and all over the place
in French postcards after World War I
like water streaming down Zeus
like the concept of optimism when it entered human history

like the simile when it said Do not end your poem with me
I am not like The End I am like a doorway
that leads from one thing

to Cincinnati, and who
am I to argue with a simile
I am a man of constant similes
that buzz and jumble as I walk
then shift and ramble as I buzz and jumble
At any moment the similes can line up
to form the log cabin Lincoln
is said to have built with his own similes
I am like a president
I am like a stove
I am President Stove I will chop down
the cherry tree over there on that page
But someone else is already chopping it down
a boy with a mad grin on his face
a glint of impish fire atop his head
Those cherries were too red!
So much for history
History that rolls above us like an onrushing storm cloud
while we below knit booties and adjust our earmuffs

Young Bentley bent over his microscope
and clicked the shutter of his box camera
thus taking the first photographic portrait of a snowflake
which is how he became known as "Snowflake" Bentley

Outside the blizzard came in sideways
like a wall of arrows
That is all you need to know about Snowflake Bentley

Who else would you like to know about?
Whom! Whom! not Who!
There actually was a great Chinese actor named Wang Whom
who immigrated to the United States in the mid-nineteenth
    century
and found fame and fortune in the theaters of San Francisco
due mainly to his ability to allow his head to detach
from his body and float up and disappear into the dark
The curtain would close to great applause
and when it opened his head was back
but his body was in two halves split right down the middle
Wang Whom never revealed his magic secrets
even to the beautiful young women who lined up toward him
like iron filings toward a magnet
powerful enough to lift President Stove out of his chair
and give him life again as a mountain
struck repeatedly by lightning
That is all you need to know about Wang Whom

Now for some commentary on things that are always horizontal
The earth is always lying down on itself
and whirling
It is totally relaxed and happy to let everything happen to it
as if it were the wisest person who ever lived

the one who never got up from bed
because the bed flew around everywhere anyone would want
    to go
and had arms and hands and legs and feet
that were those of the wise horizontal bed-person

Lines indicating very fast movement are horizontal
because the horizon is so fast it is just an idea:
Now you see it now you are it
and then ninety-nine percent of every beautiful thing you
    ever knew
escaped and went back out into the world
where you vaguely remembered it: your mother's smile
in the glint of sunlight on the chrome of a passing car,
her tears in a gust of wind, her apron in the evening air

as if she were a milkmaid standing in Holland
while those silver and gray clouds billowing across the sky
over to scarlet and burning violet tinged with gold
just for her and that one moment.

You are next in line, which is exciting,
which is why life is exciting: every moment is another line
you're next in. Or maybe not, for what about when
you don't know what "line" is and "next"? A goat
comes up close and stares at your sleeping face.
The instant you wake up it turns into a statue
that starts out a goat and ends up a banjo,

something you can neither milk nor play.
But it doesn't matter because you started out a man
and ended up a pile of leaves in a different story.
In the library the other piles are saying Shush, they know
it is late autumn, they can tell by the ruddier cheeks
of the girls who come in and, when they see their books
    are overdue,
stamp their feet in a fit of pique.
They are so cute
that some of the leaf piles shamble across the floor toward
    their dresses,
but the girls laugh and throw their hair around and dash away.
If only you weren't a pile of leaves, you would run after them
    and throw yourself on them
like a miracle!

That's what it used to be like to be fourteen and surrounded
by miracles that never happened.
At fifteen the miracles started to crackle and at sixteen
they were positively scary—Look, a miracle on the ceiling!
By seventeen a miracle was a car you could ride in
and then one year later drive beyond the limits of consciousness.
The tapioca pudding was there.
You ate it.
The tapioca pudding was gone
but there too.
May I have some more anything?
Why, my fine young man, you can have anything

you want. Here, have this mountain!

Oof, it's too heavy! Do you have a smaller one?

No, only a larger one.

Then no mountain will I have today

and as for the future I cannot say

because I have no idea where I would ever put a mountain.

But, young man, you will become President Stove!

I will? But I don't want to be a president or a stove,

I want to glue a president *to* a stove.

Then go right ahead. Here is the glue.

Now go find a president and a stove.

Bed

There's a saying
"You can't make the bed you're lying in."
Actually you can,
though it takes a bit of practice,
and when you've finished
it is nice to lie there
as part of the bed. But soon
you have the urge to move
that surges up against the urge
to keep the bed as is and you
become a battleground.
Before this point it's best
to slip out twixt the sheets
and go about your day,
the figure from a Japanese screen
who was there only a moment.

The Breakfast Nook

If I had a cup of coffee
as strong as a hammer
I would drink it so fast
that nails would fly
out of my face and
into the wall of
your silence onto
which we could hang
a picture of the cup,
the hammer, and
the nails, and we
could then have a
cup of hammers and
a nail of coffee
and a lion would
come in and roar
so loud that it
would scare you
until you saw
that it was really
a board of sugar
and a saw of cream.
Would you tell me
your secret then?

The Stapler

When my mother died
she left very little: old clothes,
modest furniture, dishes, some
change, and that was about it.
Except for the stapler. I found it
in a drawer stuffed with old bills
and bank statements. Right off
I noticed how easily it penetrated
stacks of paper, leaving no bruise
on the heel of my hand.
It worked so well I brought it home,
along with a box of staples, from
which only a few of the original 5000
were missing. The trick is remembering
how to load it—it takes me several minutes
to figure it out each time, but I persist until
Oh yes, that's it! Somewhere in all this
my mother is spread out and floating
like a mist so fine it can't be seen,
an idea of wafting, the opposite of stapler.

Different Kinds of Ink

Inchiostro is a long way to go
for *ink*, but when you get there
it is darker and more liquid and glistening
than anything you could have imagined,
you with your fables and epics, flourishing
signatures and official documents,
and drawings of beasts of the sea.
Only the squid can eject such darkness
when he hastens to flee your liquid writing,
for he squirts at his deepest level: he
is a *calamaro* and he knows you will try
to eat him, which he does not agree to,
for he must go make more *inchiostro,*
which is how he writes: all inside himself.
You have your dark and human tales
but you will never have his.

Sketch

I wonder what Clive van den Berg
is doing right now. I'll bet he's surmising
as he peers perceptively at his new drawings
though in the back of his head there
is a drawing of lunch outdoors in the shade
at a table spread with the finest little things
all tasty and symmetrical, so he adds
some shading and pepper and the outlines
of Zoë and Ingrid as a breeze rises
and falls like the edge of the tablecloth
that suggests heaven and then settles
back down into tableclothness, which is heaven
for the tablecloth and those of us who are us.

Aubade

New as a baby who has an idea for the first time
while rolling down a hill in a land no one
has ever stepped foot on, and as bright as the eyes
of a man who found himself mysteriously shot
up into the air where he hovered before chirping,
and as absolutely confident as the patient
that the crazed dentist will not hurt her, despite
the roaring chainsaw thirsty to rip and tear—
is how I am each day for a split second before
I remember what a lowly worm I am,
lifting the front of my long body to poke softly
at the air that is still fresh with dew and night.

Do You Like It?

We now take the next
step into the forest of
the imagination that William
Shakespeare walked
into when he wrote plays such
as *As You Like It,* so dark green
were those woods and filled
with fairies and enchantment
that, like sounds offstage,
are hovering near, hovering near
the hut where you have taken refuge
and the deer stand stock still because
they might have heard something
that could harm them, then look down
and go on grazing. You stop for a moment
to think of how scared you would be
if you were being introduced
to the actual William Shakespeare.
His dark eyes penetrate your head.
You look down. His shoes
make you feel like screaming.

Drive

When the cowboys sang
Get along, little dogie,

I knew they were addressing
small cows, I mean calves,

but in the back of my mind
I saw small dogs, I mean puppies,

loping alongside the herd
that mooed especially hard

when the music came up
and painted the Old West

in all its wide marvelous expansive
day and night affirmation of

sheer existence, in which even
a little dogie had a part to play,

doggy too.

Slight Foxing

The split infinitive was discovered and named in the nineteenth century. Nineteenth-century writers seem to have made greater use of this construction than earlier writers; the frequency of occurrence attracted the disapproving attention of grammarians, many of whom thought it to be a modern corruption (one commentator blamed it on Byron). In fact *to* was originally limited to use with the gerund and not until the twelfth century did it become attached to the infinitive. By the fourteenth century writers were occasionally separating *to* and the verb with an adverb; the practice went unnoticed until the nineteenth century.

—*Webster's Ninth New Collegiate Dictionary*

It's a big beautiful omelet made of children.

—Fragonard, referring to his painting *The Swarm of Love*

Before, behind, between, above, below.

—John Donne, "Elegy xix: To His Mistress Going to Bed"

Using an attribute to illustrate the point that attributes are not attributes in and of themselves is not so good as using a nonattribute to illustrate the point. Using a horse to illustrate the

point that a (white) horse is not a horse (as such) is not so good
as using nonhorses to illustrate the point. Actually the universe is
but an attribute; all things are but a horse.

> —Chuang Tzu, in *Sources of Chinese Tradition*

Mum

> —Word spelled out in flowers on a grave near an
> abandoned village on Achill Island, Ireland

History vomited up George W. Bush so he could defecate on the
human spirit.

> —Wall graffito, New York City

Seán Ó Neachtain . . . in *Stair Éamuinn Uí Chléire (The Story of
Eamon O'Clery)* . . . evolved a strange lingo which, two centuries
before Joyce, trembled on the brink of *Finnegans Wake:* "and 'tis
name to him, old hog son foal, and he is in the house of your ear
handsome seldom hundred sick . . ."

> —Declan Kiberd in *The Oxford History of Ireland*

To my surprise the heaven in my heart leaped into your eyes.

> —From the song "Remember When," words by Buck Ram

The day will come when your life will seem to have lasted
an instant.

—Unknown source

The acquisition of voluntary muscle movement, i.e., the fact that
the ego discovers . . . that its conscious will can control the body,
may well be the basic experience at the root of all magic.

—Erich Neumann, *The Origins and History of Consciousness*

Abraham Lincoln was born in a log cabin that he built with his
own hands.

—Unidentified schoolchild

We've gone to a lot of trouble to be humanity. It seems odd to
throw it away.

—Something Kenneth Koch could have said

Blink

I don't mean that there's a way to reach that high
and say anything to or for you, it's
that an impulse is darting around
in search of something that can happen
or might if we were to happen to float
through some bright rectangle standing up
into cool rooms whose surfaces are
radiant with the way you used to be,
girl giggling atop my shoulders with
sweet mischief in your glinting
and it rises again, this hand, as if
in blessing, to draw a misty figure in the air
and disappear when we most wanted it
which is forever.

Don't we know better?
Why do we await this momentary wafting that
flares up the petals of a tulip when
that voice is leaning toward
the larger outline things slip through
on their way to lightness in the light
that grows when the angel doesn't look lost
and doesn't even walk on the air it's in
in perfect symmetry that lasts for an instant
because you blinked and now it's paint so blink again.

Bird's Eye

You can use words
to clear the space where words
clutter up your view, and there's

the cottage with thatched roof
and a wisp of smoke that shows
the roof has just caught fire,

with peasants in the fields
on this, a harvest day,
their ruddy cheeks and snaggle teeth.

They scythe and bind and call
across the field, "Olaf, you nut,
come sit in the shade

and have your supper," but he
scythes on and on, for he is angry
at the gods today and in

a mood for cutting, unaware
the sky has sent a spark
to visit his abode.

But now I'll clutter up the view
again, and close your ears
to the sound of distant peasant laughter.

Now You See It

What you don't see
helps you see what
you do see: the keyhole
sharpens the thrill
in your brain,
even if there is
no one
in the room,
shadows
wafting across
the white sheets
as a song drifts in
the window,
her voice so pure
you can see
the face it rises from,
for what you see
helps you see what
you don't see.

Hercules

stood on the hillock
and roared just
because he was
Hercules. The waves
below crashed below
the churning sky.
It would have
been Christmas
but it was too
early in history,
therefore no
gifts for him.
But he didn't
need a gift:
he was Hercules!
An outline was
always around him—
in case he went
away there would
be a drawing left.
That's what we
see now. If you
want to hear him
roar, listen.

Bible Study

And they entered the ark
two by two

except for the studs
which were two by four

The hammers and nails
got on board too

Everything that existed
got on board

to go to a new place
and build an exact replica

of the old place
after the flood subsided.

And subside it did
so that later

a new one could rise
again, like the old flood.

The new flood would say
Ha ha! and

The new Noah would say
Ho ho!

Elegy for No One

Time passes slowly when you're lost in paradise,
then gradually slows down to a disappearance

but only for a moment, as if inside a footstep
that pauses on the stair to wait for its shadow

to catch up, for it had not yet vanished as
the other had, and you have the idea you

wanted to have had when
the candlelight took away the distance,

leaving only the residue of dimness and fading
falling to one side and off. Time goes past or you

go past time, the outcome is the same if you think
of it that way, but if you don't think at all

the footstep will have existed on the stair
without you, as it always has, and perfectly so.

C Note

Hokusai, or
as they used to spell it,
Ho-Ku-Sai
painted 100
views of Fuji,
then stopped.
No 101
for him!
And I say
Bully!
because
I've written
99 poems
this summer,
not counting
this one.

Bastille Day

The first time I saw Paris
I went to see where the Bastille
had been, and though
I saw the column there
I was too aware that
the Bastille was not there:
I did not know how
to see the emptiness.
People go to see
the missing Twin Towers
and seem to like feeling
the lack of something.
I do not like knowing
that my mother no longer
exists, or the feeling
of knowing. Excuse me
for comparing my mother
to large buildings. Also
for talking about absence.
The red and gray sky
above the rooftops
is darkening and the inhabitants
are hastening home for dinner.
I hope to see you later.

Ron Padgett is a celebrated memoirist, translator, and "thoroughly American poet, coming sideways out of Whitman, Williams, and New York Pop with a Tulsa twist" (Peter Gizzi). His poetry has been translated into sixteen languages and has appeared in *The Best American Poetry, Poetry 180, The Norton Anthology of Postmodern American Poetry,* and *The Oxford Book of American Poetry,* as well as on Garrison Keillor's *Writer's Almanac.* Padgett's recent books include *Joe: A Memoir of Joe Brainard,* a collection of collaborative poems *If I Were You,* and a translation of *Prose Poems* by Pierre Reverdy.

In addition to receiving grants and fellowships from the Guggenheim Foundation, the Foundation for Contemporary Arts, the National Endowment for the Arts, and the American Academy of Arts and Letters, Padgett was made an Officer in the Order of Arts and Letters by the French government. He lives in New York City and Calais, Vermont. Visit his web site at www.ronpadgett.com.

COLOPHON

How to Be Perfect was designed at Coffee House Press,
in the historic warehouse district of downtown Minneapolis.
Fonts include Fournier and Gill Sans.

FUNDER ACKNOWLEDGMENT

Coffee House Press is an independent nonprofit literary publisher. Our books are made possible through the generous support of grants and gifts from many foundations, corporate giving programs, individuals, and through state and federal support. Coffee House Press receives general operating support from the Minnesota State Arts Board, through an appropriation by the Minnesota State Legislature and from the National Endowment for the Arts, and major general operating support from the McKnight Foundation, and from the Target Foundation. Coffee House also receives support from: an anonymous donor; the Elmer and Eleanor Andersen Foundation; the Buuck Family Foundation; the Patrick and Aimee Butler Family Foundation; Stephen and Isabel Keating; the Lenfestey Family Foundation; Rebecca Rand; the law firm of Schwegman, Lundberg, Woessner & Kluth, P.A.; the James R. Thorpe Foundation; the Archie D. and Bertha H. Walker Foundation; the Woessner Freeman Family Foundation; Wood-Rill Foundation; and many other generous individual donors.

This activity is made possible in part by a grant from the Minnesota State Arts Board, through an appropriation by the Minnesota State Legislature and a grant from the National Endowment for the Arts. MINNESOTA STATE ARTS BOARD

TARGET.

To you and our many readers across the country,
we send our thanks for your continuing support.

Good books are brewing at coffeehousepress.org